More Graffiti

Devotions for guys

To Todd with love
from Mom & Dad
1-7-89

Remember your life verse:
"For God has not given us the
spirit of fear, but of power,
and of love, and of a sound
mind." 2 Timothy 1:7

More Graffiti

Devotions for guys

J. David Schmidt

Power Books

Fleming H. Revell Company
Old Tappan, New Jersey

Library of Congress Cataloging in Publication Data

Schmidt, J. David (John David)
  More graffiti: devotions for guys.

  "Power books."
  Summary: Offers sixty discussions, each with a relevant
Bible verse, on topics such as peer pressure, shyness,
self-worth, parents, sex and love, and other aspects of
daily life.
  1. Adolescent boys—Prayer-books and devotions—
English. [1. Prayer-books and devotions. 2. Christian
life] I. Title.
BV4855.S36 1984   242'.632   83-24523
ISBN 0-8007-5142-6

BEFORE YOU READ
THIS BOOK,
READ THIS PAGE

Okay. So you've got this devotional book called *More Graffiti*. Now what? You *could* use it to club your little brother into submission or prop up other books your mother has bought you—or you might use it as a plate for some late-night pizza.

Of course, you *could* try reading the devotions inside. They've been written to help you and to show you how the Bible has down-to-earth advice for some of the tough questions you face. *You* know you're unique. But in these pages you'll see that others your age are facing the same problems you face. The important thing to keep in mind is that God wants to be your Friend and help you grow as a Christian.

It's tough to be a Christian today. I hope as you read you'll see that God has given you lots of help in the Bible.

Hang in there,

J. David

CONTENTS

More Graffiti

Devotions for guys

1

HANDLING HURTS

"Up until last year about the worst thing that ever happened to me was that I got turned down for a date to the Spring Fling. Then, not too long ago, we found out my dad is dying of cancer. I mean, like, I came unglued inside.**"**

Hurts and pain come in all shapes and sizes. Your best friend moves away. You break up with your girl friend. You lose a race in the state finals. All of these kinds of things have pain associated with them. The interesting thing about pain or hurt is that it's so intensely personal. What seems like a small hurt to one person may actually be a large hurt to another. Thankfully, for most people your age, there are not a lot of the big hurts in life; most hurts are passing. But what if there *are* big hurts? What if your dad *is* dying of cancer, or your mom and dad *are* getting divorced? Or your sister died two years ago? What strength do you draw on then? How do you get over that feeling of aloneness?

Here is something worth remembering when the hurts of life crowd in on you: "The righteous cry out, and the Lord hears them; he delivers them from all their troubles. The Lord is close to the brokenhearted and saves those who are crushed in spirit" (Psalms 34:17,18).

When you hurt as a Christian, you have the freedom and the right to call on God for help. Sending a message to God, when you can't see Him is really a mystery, but millions of Christians will tell you that God does come close to those who have broken hearts. That doesn't mean God takes away all the trouble and hurt; it does mean He will make the pain more bearable. Some guys act like nothing hurts them—from getting turned down for a date to their dad dying. They feel obligated to be macho. But when guys are really honest, they admit that they hurt too.

Throughout your life you will experience hurts of all shapes and sizes. You don't have to hide that. In fact, the more willing you are to admit that you do hurt, the easier it is for God to come and help you.

FANTASY WORLD

2

"Yeah, I think about sex a lot. Really, in today's world how can you not?**"**

For most guys, it doesn't take much to get them thinking about sex. A girl can cross her legs or smile a certain way, and the machinery that cranks out sexual thoughts starts to work. Do you think it matters to God what you think? Does it really matter what you think? The fact is, it does. And God has some ideas on the subject. "Finally, brothers, whatever is true, whatever is noble, whatever is right, whatever is pure, whatever is lovely, whatever is admirable—if anything is excellent or praiseworthy—think about such things" (Philippians 4:8).

In this verse, God gives us some guidelines on what to think about. Frankly, there's not much room for lusty thoughts about girls. What did God have in mind here? Basically one thing: God knows that *the first line of defense* against problems in your life is good thinking. It should be pretty clear to you that any time you have sinned sexually, it's been because first your thoughts went down a certain path and then your actions followed. By thinking clearly and cleanly, you have a line of defense against problems in life. Most of the time, it's easier and more fun *not* to think about the right stuff. Thinking about sex is a part of life, but God set this standard up for our good so that we would be balanced not only in *how much* we think about sex, but *how* we think about it as well. How's your thought life? Most of those thoughts that just pop into your mind about girls, you can't do much about, but how long you dwell on those thoughts is your choice. Ask God to help you establish a first line of defense by helping you think cleanly.

3

LEADERSHIP
QUALITIES

"It always seems like the most popular or good-looking guys get elected as class president. It really makes me wonder whether there's room for normal people in leadership.**"**

Who gets elected in your school as class president or captain of the football team? The person with the most friends, the nicest clothes? The person who lives in the right neighborhood and has his own car? Is it the most friendly person? The most gifted person? Oftentimes, our culture tends to put people in places of leadership because of outward gifts and abilities. You could say they have charisma. Somehow we've come to expect that these people have unusual gifts and abilities to lead others. The fact is, though, people with lots of friends, nice clothes, and good looks don't always make the best leaders. In fact, Jesus had a different idea about who makes good leaders. "Jesus called them together and said, 'You know that those who are regarded as rulers of the Gentiles lord it over them, and their high officials exercise authority over them. Not so with you. Instead, whoever wants to become great among you must be your servant, and whoever wants to be first must be slave of all. For even the Son of Man did not come to be served, but to serve, and to give his life as a ransom for many'" (Mark 10:42–45).

This is one of those verses in the Bible that is confusing at first glance. How can you be a servant and still be a leader? *In your attitude.* Many politicians live and act like being leaders is something they deserve. The Bible makes it pretty clear that real leaders serve others. They have an attitude of helping others. They advance in life through hard work, not by stepping on other people to get to a higher level. No matter where you work in life, whether you marry or not, people will look to you for leadership. Someday it might be ten employees, it might be your wife or daughter, or someone in the Sunday school class. Don't be fooled into thinking that the best leaders in those spots are those who look good or have charisma. God and people in this world are looking for and need leaders who serve.

WHAT DOES A CHRISTIAN LOOK LIKE?

"Sometimes I wonder what a real Christian looks like. I have a lot of friends who call themselves Christians, but brother, you'd never know it by the way they act."

What does a real Christian look like in today's world? Does he carry his Bible to school and pray in the cafeteria? Or is he somebody who shows up in church on Sunday, but the rest of the week will go drinking with the guys or mess around with girls? Sometimes it's hard to know what a Christian really looks like. When people call themselves Christians, yet live differently than we do, it gets confusing. It makes it difficult to know whether we're right or they're right. Here's what the Bible says on the subject: "Therefore, if anyone is in Christ, he is a new creation; the old has gone, the new has come!" (2 Corinthians 5:17.)

The Bible makes it clear. We don't have to be confused about what a Christian really looks like. In a nutshell, a Christian is someone whose life is different, cleaner today than what it used to be. What's going on now in his life is different from the past. Another way you could say it is that the world thinks a

19

certain way, but Christians think a different way. It's not that Christians look so different, or live so differently. It's the fact that a Christian has more of a desire to do what God wants than what he wants. That doesn't mean he won't sin. It does mean, though, that the power and the fun of sin is broken in his life. Sometimes we have the mistaken impression that when we become Christians, God wants to take away all the fun and all the good things in life. It's not true. What God does want to do is to take away the power enjoyable things in life have over us. He wants to replace it with joy and peace in our lives that is lasting. Other Christians can confuse us when we look to them to tell us what a Christian really is. The Bible makes it clear: A Christian is somebody whose new life is different from his old life. It's not how you dress, whether you pray in the cafeteria, or what you do on a Friday night that really counts. What really counts is to have faith in God even when you can't see Him and a life-style that is different from the way you lived before you knew God.

5

JOCKS

"I got hit so hard I thought I'd see stars. I'm sure glad I had my jock on."

Protection. It's sure a nice thing to have when you're hit hard playing football, or you catch a line drive in the infield. Protection in sports not only makes the games you play safer, but a lot more fun, too. With protection, you can relax a little more and concentrate on the plays in the game. The Christian life is a lot like a sport such as football, where protection not only makes the game safer, but makes it more enjoyable. The Bible talks about some protection you need in life. "Finally, be strong in the Lord and his mighty power. Put on the full armor of God so that you can take your stand against the devil's schemes" (Ephesians 6:10,11).

The armor the Bible talks about is symbolic. But it's interesting to note that the armor of God and a football uniform have some similarities. Both cover the parts of your body that are most vulnerable to injury, and both grew out of years of experience. The parts of today's football uniform are based on years of playing the game and of research into how to best protect a man. God has provided a symbolic armor for you. He has given you His Word—the Bible—to provide guidance for life's tough questions. He's given you a church or a team where you can get support. And He's given you access to Him, the Coach, at any time through prayer. Just like in football, the armor God supplies you is not designed to take the fun out of the game. Rather it's designed to make the game—in this case your life—safer and more enjoyable.

6

FRIENDS' INFLUENCE

❝I know they don't think like I do, but what's the big deal? A guy's gotta have some friends in this world.**❞**

One of the most important things to a teenager is his friends. Sometimes you probably feel your friends know you and understand you better than anyone else, even your family. Actually, that's quite natural. But what happens when your friends think differently than you, live differently than you, and have different values? What kind of an influence do they have on your life? Here's what the Bible says about friendships. "Do not be misled: 'Bad company corrupts good character.'" (1 Corinthians 15:33).

Did you catch the significance of that? It's the bad company that has more influence than the good. You'd think it would be just the opposite, that good people would persuade bad company to change their ways, but it's not that way. When you spend a lot of time with bad company—whatever that means to you—or engage in activities that bad company appreciates, it puts you in a compromising spot. You may believe you're strong enough to resist, but it's not likely. If you're with bad company, and that bad company decides to play chicken on a highway, and you get in an accident, you may be innocent, but you'll still get hurt. Good friendships are critical in life.

God doesn't expect us to hang out only with the schoolies, or the holy people, or by ourselves. Are your friends building you up or often asking you to compromise what you know is right? Take this verse as a warning. Find a balance of friendships in your life.

7

IF ONLY ...

❝I'd say my biggest problem is sex—no, getting along with my parents. I don't know. It's one of the two.❞

What is your biggest problem? Everyone thinks he's got one. For some people, it's handling sex. For other people, it's loneliness. For someone else, it's getting along with his parents or his brother. The fact is, everyone has some problem that seems bigger than other problems, that troubles him. Even Christians struggle with one sin more than others. Big problems don't solve themselves overnight. We live in an imperfect world where it takes time to work out problems. "Therefore, since we are surrounded by such a great cloud of witnesses, let us throw off everything that hinders and the sin that so easily entangles, and let us run with perseverance the race marked out for us" (Hebrews 12:1).

Believe it or not, a lot of people we read about in the Bible—Moses, Noah, Abraham, John, Peter—struggled with some sin in their lives too. Yet God still talked to them and worked with them in their lives. The thing to keep in mind is that everyone has one sin that easily gets to him more than others. The key for everyone, and you, is to persevere. Paul used a race as the example. In some ways, it's like a cross-country race. It takes a lot of perseverance to win. The only way you can persevere and win over a big problem in your life is to do what the next verse says, and that is, fix your eyes on Jesus. Or, in other words, talk to Jesus and rely on Him for strength.

8

COME ON, MOM

❝I know cleaning up my room is my responsibility, but I can sure think of a lot of other things I'd rather do with my Saturday mornings.**❞**

Cleaning up your room—what a hassle. You know it's your responsibility. After all, you made the mess. Still, when you get right down to it, it's a pain to have to take the time to clean up your room. Seems like there are a lot more important things to do with your life. By now, you have probably figured out that there are any number of ways to clean up your room. You know putting stuff back in its place is the best way, but how many times does that option win out? Another way you can clean up your room is to hide things under the bed or in the closet. That's a good option until you're in a hurry someday and need to find something super quick. A third option is to rearrange everything in your room—you don't really throw anything away. You just arrange things into nice neat piles. That's a great option until you start to collect so much stuff you have to make a path between your bed and your closet.

Sometimes, guys try to clean up their lives the same way they try to clean up their rooms. They make mistakes and then try to hide or cover up those mistakes by burying them. Sometimes guys rearrange their lives, never dealing with a bad attitude or something they did wrong. Lots of times, the best option—putting stuff back in its place and throwing some things away—is an option people rarely exercise. They pile up a bad attitude toward their sister or their dad. They might keep a dirty magazine underneath the mattress—never really throw it away and once in a while go back to it. Maybe they told a lie or cheated on a test and wanted to make it right, but just never did it. How about you? Have you cleaned up your life lately? And when you did, *how* did you clean it up? Did you rearrange everything in your life? Did you save some things, trying to hide them? Or did you clean up your life by putting things back in their place and throwing some things away?

Here's some advice from the Bible that's worth looking at. "Since we have these promises, dear friends, let us purify ourselves from everything that contaminates body and spirit, perfecting holiness out of reverence for God" (2 Corinthians 7:1). God knows that it's tough to stay clean in a dirty world. It's tough to keep the rooms of your life in order in a world that's based on wild and crazy values. But we have a promise in the Bible that God will help us as we do our part to stay clean. Cleaning out the rooms in your life is a good exercise. It's something every Christian has to do occasionally. The great thing about cleaning out the rooms of your life is that once you do, you'll be able to make more sense out of life. Do you ever notice how good you feel after you've cleaned up your room, and how the room feels new? Well, the same thing happens when you clean out some of the "rooms" in your life. There's a freshness and a new start about going to God and saying, "God, help me get rid of the things in my life that bog me down, that make my life messy." How about you? Have you cleaned out the rooms of your life lately?

9 FRIENDS' IMPORTANCE

"What's the most valuable thing in my life right now? I'd say my friends."

What's the most valuable thing in your life right now? Your friends, your family, your good health, your brain? Lots of teenagers today feel that being popular is the most valuable thing in life. They feel secure about themselves and their identity when they feel their friends like them. But did you know that when somebody becomes popular it's sometimes because weak people need to lean on someone they think is stronger or better than they. People who have strong values and their own identity don't need to be close friends with popular kids. They are strong on their own. How strong are you? Do you have a goal and purpose in life other than having friends or feeling good? One of the good things about being a Christian is that it helps you feel good about yourself, but for different reasons than being popular. The Bible says, "For whoever finds me finds life and receives favor from the Lord" (Proverbs 8:35).

If you are a Christian—in other words, if you walk with God—your life is going a different direction than the lives of most of your friends at school. Friendships and having a good time, staying in shape, making the team, or getting a part in the school play, are all important, even to Christians. But when compared to the most important thing in life—knowing God—these things become a part of life rather than all of life. Any weak person can be a part of a clique and be popular. But it takes a strong person, a person with character, to be different. You want to know what's valuable in life? What's really valuable is to know God personally and to take the good things of life and make them count for Him.

SKILLS IN LIFE

10

❝I talked to the guidance counselor yesterday. He said I had to have at least one marketable skill to make it in this life. The trouble is, I don't know what I'm good at, and I haven't been that successful so far in my life as it is.**❞**

Did you ever wonder if you have what it takes to make it in life? Wondering whether or not we've got something going in life is a question that troubles everyone, and if the answer doesn't come quickly, some days, we wonder if we're worth anything at all. Here's an interesting quote to think about: "Who you are is not defined by what you do or where you've been or where you're going. If you know God personally, your worth in life has already been determined." Here's what the Bible says: "For I am convinced that neither death nor life, neither angels nor demons, neither the present nor the future, nor any powers, neither height nor depth, nor anything else in all creation, will be able to separate us from the love of God that is in Christ Jesus our Lord" (Romans 8:38,39).

Believe it or not, God won't ever love you any more or any less than He does right now, today. Your worth has already been determined. Think about it; there are over 4 billion people on the face of the earth, yet the Bible says that absolutely nothing, not sheer numbers of people, not anything you've done, not any place you've ever been, nothing can separate you from God's love. What that means is that you have value, that you're worth something not only to God, but to the world and to the people around you. You may not be good at something visible like sports, or have good looks. You may come from a poor family, or you may even have a few zits. But the point is that you have qualities for doing certain things quite well. You just may not know them at the moment. You may not wake up every morning feeling like you've got skills or abilities, but the fact is you do have something good to give others. Ask God to show you what you're good at and remember: Nothing you've ever done, said, been, or thought can separate you from God's love. In God's eyes, you are valuable.

HOLDING ON

"My youth group leader talked about self-control last week. It sounds so boring, like to be self-controlled makes life a drag. I know I've got to have more of it, but does self-control have to hurt so bad?**"**

Self-control is one of those qualities of life everyone wants to have, but when it gets down to living life on a day-to-day basis, it's pretty tough to find. Jesus told an interesting story about a farmer who scattered seeds, some of which fell on a path, some on rocky places, some fell among thorns, and some fell on good soil. Here is what He said about the seeds that fell on rocks: "What was sown on rocky places is the man who hears the word and at once receives it with joy. But since he has no root, he lasts only a short time. When trouble or persecution comes because of the word, he quickly falls away" (Matthew 13:20,21).

One of the reasons you might lack self-control in your life is wrapped up in those two verses. Let's say you hear something you know to be true, like reading dirty magazines is bad for you, or watching too much television doesn't help you develop in life. You know both of those things are true. If you heard them at church you might get excited about them. But then when you've got homework and a good show comes on TV, or a friend offers to lend you some dirty magazines for the night, that's when the test of self-control begins. The guy who wins those battles, and a lot of other ones, is the guy who has roots. His roots go down deep in his life so that when confronted with a choice to do right or wrong, he can make the right choice the majority of the time. That's the whole point of self-control. Self-control is making the right decisions the majority of the time. The Bible makes it clear we're never going to be perfect in life. What Jesus asks is that you work hard toward eliminating sin in your life. One of the best ways to do that is to have self-control so that *you*—not your body—control what you see, what you think, and where you go. Self-control is getting to the point where you can call on God to help you when you're faced with tough choices. God wants you to have self-control, not to spoil your life, but to help you make good choices when faced with a decision to do right or wrong. The more you bring your feelings and your body in line and work hard keeping your time and your life disciplined, the more victories you'll have over sin.

12

THINK AGAIN

"If I was really honest about it, I'd say my thought life is like a game of Donkey Kong. I'm always struggling to get to a higher level."

A lot of people feel that way when it comes to their minds and what they think about. It's pretty tough not to think about sex when you're hit over the head with it a dozen times a day in magazines, on television, and in songs. The Bible makes it clear that if your thought life is weak or shaky, you are more vulnerable than ever to sin. Here's some advice that's worth remembering: "Finally, brothers, whatever is true, whatever is noble, whatever is right, whatever is pure, whatever is lovely, whatever is admirable—if anything is excellent or praiseworthy—think about such things" (Philippians 4:8).

If you went through that list you'd see that's a tall order. It's hard to think pure thoughts or the right thing all day long, but when you stop to think about it, there has to be a good reason why God would give us such advice. There are certain things that aren't on that list—thoughts about some fold-out you saw recently, a fantasy with some girl you know, telling your dad off in your mind, picturing a way to get even with somebody you don't like. Nasty thoughts, but they're bound to cross your mind some time or another. God gave us a list of things to think about, things that are good and lovely and admirable or excellent, not to cramp our mental style, but to help guide us away from the things in life that might tempt us. God knows the progression better than you do. First you think about sin, then you go and do the sin. God knows that if He can help you be careful about what you think, then sin is further away. But if your thought life is bad, then sin is that much closer. Sin starts in your thought life. If you want to win the war against sin in your life, you've got to start with good thinking. The question is, who owns your mind? How would you answer that question? You or God?

13

TEMPTATION

> **"**I know the Bible talks about being tempted and temptation, but I hardly ever hear little voices whispering at me. I can't always tell when I'm being tempted.**"**

Could you spot temptation in your life when it happens? In fact, what does temptation look like in today's world? Somehow we always think of temptation as being the big things like being tempted to go to a topless bar, telling a lie to our parents, or getting blasted at a party. Actually, temptation can be and usually is a lot more subtle than what you might first think. Here's what the Bible says: "When tempted, no one should say, 'God is tempting me.' For God cannot be tempted by evil, nor does he tempt anyone; but each one is tempted when, by his own evil desire, he is dragged away and enticed. Then, after desire has conceived, it gives birth to sin; and sin, when it is full-grown, gives birth to death" (James 1:13–15).

It's good to be reminded, but most of us know that God doesn't tempt us with things that are going to hurt us. What we usually forget, though, is that temptation starts in really small ways. It starts with just a small desire to feel good, to have a good time with our friends, or to be just a little nasty. These small desires, though, if let alone, grow and in the right circumstances, those desires flare up and grow rapidly to a point where we give in to them. As a result, we sin. And if we sin long enough, a part of us dies.

You can apply this to any issue in life; let's say you have an argument with your parents. During the argument, you have just a small desire to be right, and for them to see your point of view. Given the right circumstances, and enough arguments with your parents, that little attitude of wanting to be right can grow to the point where you get really ticked off and tell your dad to go to hell. That kind of bitterness and anger started clear back with just a tiny little attitude. It's the same with booze or sex. It always starts with just one little drink or just one kiss on the cheek. Temptation occasionally comes into our lives in big ways, but most of the time it starts with that little desire that grows larger and larger until ultimately it becomes a sin. Many of the desires in life come from God because they're basically good. There's no sin in wanting to be with other people or to be held close by someone of the opposite sex. But when those desires are taken too far, that's when trouble sets in. Ask God today to help you spot temptation in your life. Do you know that as your Friend, God has His arm around you the whole day through? Why not ask Him to make you sensitive to His hand on your shoulder as He works to guide you away from the things in life that will only harm you.

14 PRACTICAL RELIGION

❝I get so sick and tired of having Bible verses quoted to me. Don't do this and don't do that. Christianity seems like one big list of do's and don'ts.**❞**

It's sad, but many Christians really think that Christianity is a lot of do's and don'ts, and they live miserable lives never knowing the friendship and the great things that can happen when they see Christianity for what it really is. Knowing God personally and walking with Him can be one of the best things that ever happened to you. But if you feel that being a Christian means following a long list of do's and don'ts, you're living with the wrong impression. It's true that God has some guidelines for our lives, but those guidelines that He sets out in the Bible are not to burden us or to make our lives miserable and unhappy. They're designed to protect our emotions, minds, and bodies from the hurt, pain, and guilt that comes from breaking certain rules. If you ever looked at the Book of Numbers in the Old Testament you'd see that God laid down lots of laws for the Israelites. He did that not because He was a dictator, but because He was working to protect His people from disease and troubled relationships with each other. Sometimes Bible-thumping

Christians will quote a verse of Scripture to scare you into doing something or scare you into not doing something. That's really not the way God intended the Bible to be used. When you read your Bible and come across a troublesome verse, you need to take a larger view, to step back one step and say, "What is God really saying to me in this verse?" God never intended Christianity to be impractical. Look at this verse: "Religion that God our Father accepts as pure and faultless is this: to look after orphans and widows in their distress and to keep oneself from being polluted by the world" (James 1:27).

That verse is, in a word, practical. Doing something nice for a widow or someone who doesn't have a parent is what God had in mind for Christianity. People around you need to see your Christianity as being active and alive and not some dead list of do's and don'ts. God wants you to have a walk with Him that is practical. Next time you hear a Christian trying to make you feel guilty with a verse of Scripture, stop and realize that the God you know has a good plan, an exciting plan for your life and that the guidelines He has given you in Scripture are designed to be practical help for you throughout your life.

15 THANKFULNESS

❝Can God be serious when He says in the Bible to thank Him for everything?**❞**

So you wrecked the car once. Another day you flunked a history test and got turned down for a date to the senior class variety show. And in all that, you're supposed to give God thanks. Right. Any Christian in his right mind would find it really difficult to give God thanks under tough circumstances. So what does the Bible mean when it says, "Be joyful always; pray continually; give thanks in all circumstances, for this is God's will for you in Christ Jesus" (1 Thessalonians 5:16–18). When things go wrong in our lives and we hurt, it's tough to be joyful or to pray or to give thanks in everything. And if you measure a normal Christian against these verses, almost every Christian fails. So what's the point of the verse? The point of the verse is simply this. It's a goal to shoot for, it's an attitude that God is saying in His Word we should have when bad things happen. When we are asked to be joyful or to pray or to give thanks when things are tough, our minds go to work and usually ask this simple question: *How can this be a good thing for me? How can I give thanks for this?* Somehow in asking that question, we wrestle with whether we really believe God. In other words, when bad things happen to us in life, they test our faith in God, they test whether we really believe God can take a bad circumstance and turn it around for good in our lives.

When the Bible says to be joyful always and to give thanks in every circumstance, it's another way of saying, "Think this thing through, this is not the end of the line." God loves you and even when this bad thing has happened to you, this storm will pass too. Out of it, God will bring something good.

16

HASSLES WITH PARENTS

"My dad is too strict. I wish he'd realize that I'm not a kid anymore."

Did you ever hear something like this from your dad: "No dates till you get your algebra grade up," or "Don't even think of showing up at dinner with jeans and a T-shirt on." Parents do overstep themselves occasionally and are too strict about some things. But did you ever stop and ask yourself why? Why are they so strict? Most of the time, parents are strict for one reason—they care about you. And they fear that some of your mistakes might get you in big trouble. Somehow when they're strict, parents feel they're helping you use your head better. That's not much consolation when you're grounded, or the car is taken away from you, or your parents make you come in before the sun sets. So how do you handle it when your parents are too strict?

The Bible gives some good advice. "Children, obey your parents in the Lord, for this is right. 'Honor your father and mother'—which is the first commandment with a promise—that it may go well with you and that you may enjoy long life on the earth" (Ephesians 6:1–3). At first glance, that may seem like a heavy-duty command. Sometimes when your parents are too strict, it's tough to honor them and to obey them. Resentment or bitterness builds up inside. One of the ways you can honor your mom and dad is to talk to your folks straight. Sit down

43

with them and tell them what you're feeling. Tell them when you think they're too strict, ask them for explanations. When you talk to your parents as an adult, it's easier for them to respond to you as an adult. Interestingly enough, the verse after the one that says "children obey your parents" says "Fathers, do not exasperate your children; instead bring them up in the training and instruction of the Lord." God put that verse in there as a warning to fathers because God knew that sometimes parents would be too strict. So in other words, it's more like a partnership. God asks parents to be careful and not to exasperate their children, and He asks children to be careful and honor their parents. God knew that healthy relationships between parents and children can benefit you all the rest of your life. As you work at being honest with your parents and honoring them you'll find that your relationships, not only with your parents but with other people, will run a lot smoother.

BLUE MOVIES

17

> **"**I've gone to a couple of R-rated movies. They always make sex seem like so much fun. It really gets confusing to know who's right, the movie producers or my parents.**"**

One of the great illusions is sex in the movies. If you believed everything you saw on the screen, you would believe that all women are beautiful and are just waiting for men to get them into bed. Today's movies make sex look like a constant high. The sad fact of the matter is, it's not true. The movies are selling you and the general public an illusion. Sometimes illusions are acceptable and good entertainment, but when it comes to sex the rules change. When real people begin to believe that sex is always like it is in the movies, trouble starts. If you're a Christian, God wants something better for you than the illusion Hollywood tries to sell you about sex.

Here's what the Bible says: "So we fix our eyes not on what is seen, but on what is unseen. For what is seen is temporary, but what is unseen is eternal" (2 Corinthians 4:18). The Bible rarely minces words, and when it comes to this issue of what really counts in life, it makes it clear. You just can't always trust what you see to be real. Sex in a magazine or in the movies is performed under highly controlled situations. Makeup, lighting, and sound effects are all added to real people to make them appear to be prettier or appear to be into it more than they really are. Much of what you see on television or at the movies is largely a controlled magic act. You can't believe it. And if you do believe that the physical expression of love is anything like Hollywood portrays it to be, you're on the road to great disappointment and confusion.

Throughout the Bible, God makes it clear that men are to honor women and to care for them, to love them and to respect them. That means your mother, your sister, your girl friend, your date. To do that, you have to look deeper than what you see on the surface. You have to see a woman as more than just a sex object. That requires you to concentrate on values you can't always see. It's natural to be physically attracted to women, it's not quite as natural to treat them with respect. But God asks you as a Christian man to do that. How far you go on a date, where you go on a date, and how much time you spend kissing or talking will tell you a lot about what you think of women. Stop and take an inventory. How are you treating the women in your life? God asks every Christian man to concentrate on a woman's qualities that are beneath the surface of her skin. Hollywood asks you to concentrate only on the skin. If you have to struggle in this, you're not alone. Millions of other men are right with you. Take some time today and ask God to help you in your own mind to concentrate on the qualities that make a woman really beautiful.

18 WISE IN YOUR OWN EYES

"You could say I pick my friends carefully. After all, people at school look up to me and I don't want to disappoint them.**"**

If you come from a good home or your parents have money or you have brains or do well in sports, God has been good to you. But what happens when a person begins to believe that he is slightly better than those around him? Here's what the Bible says: "Do you see a man wise in his own eyes? There is more hope for a fool than for him" (Proverbs 26:12).

Pride has been around as long as man has been around. It's inevitable that out of a group of people, some are going to be better at certain things than others. Not everyone can be a quarterback or a team captain or ace a history test. If you're good at something in life, really good, how do you look at yourself? The Bible says that if you think you're cool, there's more hope for somebody who has less than you have. You can always tell people who think they have more than others. They walk differently, they hold their heads higher, they drive their cars differently, they're careful who they eat lunch with or who they're seen with in public. God hates it when Christians are proud. He knows better than you know that your gifts and talents come from Him, not you. There's nothing wrong with feeling good about a victory or sharing that victory with someone you know. But there is a great difference between sharing a victory and feeling so good about your accomplishment that you begin to act proud. God hates pride. Take an inventory in your own life. How well do you handle the victories that God has given you?

19

THINKING PATTERNS

❝What does the Bible mean when it says, 'Don't conform any longer to the pattern of this world'? That verse makes it sound like having a good time is a sin.**❞**

At first glance, there *are* verses in the Bible that make being a Christian sound like a first-class drag. Here's one that seems that way: "Do not conform any longer to the pattern of this world, but be transformed by the renewing of your mind. Then you will be able to test and approve what God's will is—his good, pleasing and perfect will" (Romans 12:2).

God has never been against you having a good time in life. In fact, just the opposite is true. Better than you know, or your parents or your friends, God knows what it takes to have a good time. God knows that if you try to be a Christian one day and not be one the next, you'll be miserable, and being miserable is not part of having a good time. The world has a certain pattern to it, to good times. Many of the good times—such as getting drunk, getting high, dirty movies, dirty magazines, sex outside of marriage—all have the same philosophy behind them: Enjoy what you're doing now, and don't worry about what happens tomorrow or what the end results are. The Bible says think differently. Break that pattern in your life of "if it feels good, do it." The way to break that pattern is to change your way of thinking. It's like a game of Pac Man; the patterns you choose definitely determine whether you'll win the game or not. The same is true about your life. The Bible says if you really want to be successful and you want to know God's best for your life, you're going to have to think differently, and to do that, you'll have to renew your mind. In other words, put good things in it. It's hard to believe, but your success in life is directly dependent on how you think. If you're walking with God and reading His Word on a regular basis, God can help you find His good and pleasing will for your life.

20

WISDOM

"I want to go to college next year, but it's really been hard for me to decide what school to go to.**"**

Making good choices is something you will face for the rest of your life. Maybe it's what college to go to, or who to date, or whether you should marry someone or not. There are lots of big choices ahead of you in life, and how you handle them will determine not only the direction of your life, but really what kind of a life you'll end up having. Millions of teenagers today base their decisions simply on their feelings or what they think is the right thing to do. Lots of times they make up their mind to do something because it feels good at the time, only to find out later that they made some big mistakes.

Did you know that as a Christian, you don't have to make up your mind or make decisions by yourself? Did you know that you have Someone you can count on for help, from the simplest decision to the largest decision? Here's some good news if you're facing big decisions. "If any of you lacks wisdom, he should ask God, who gives generously to all without finding fault, and it will be given to him. But when he asks, he must believe and not doubt, because he who doubts is like a wave of the sea, blown and tossed by the wind" (James 1:5,6). When God promises something, you can count on Him to come through for you. What this verse means is that with any decision you ever have to make, you can count on God to give you help. All you have to do is ask Him. That's it, just ask Him, and believe that He can come through for you. He will give you the wisdom you need to make good decisions. Often in life, you need something more to draw on besides your own experience, your own family, or your own education. God can give you what you need and He promises to give you the wisdom you need generously. It doesn't matter where you've been or what you've done. He'll do all that for you simply because He cares about you. Who you should marry and what college you should go to are big decisions in life. You don't have to face them alone. The more you involve God in your life, in making these big decisions, the safer you'll be and the more confidence you'll have that you made the right ones.

VIDEO JUNKIE

21

❝I know this guy at school who's a video junkie. Gee, is he strange. He even saves his lunch money just to go and play the machines.**❞**

Video junkies are everywhere today. You can spot them right away when you walk into an arcade. The video junkie is usually the guy who's been on the machine an hour and a half. His hand is glued to the joy stick, his eyes bulge out. He's usually the guy who's bumming quarters from somebody or who skips out of school early just to take his chances doing battle with colored dots on a television screen. Most people are not video junkies, spending hours and hours in an arcade. But most everyone spends hours and hours—doing absolutely nothing. Wasting time seems to be part of the American way, but that sure doesn't make it right. Did you know that because you are a Christian, it matters to God how you spend the hours in your day? Here's what the Bible says: "Be very careful, then, how you live—not as unwise but as wise, making the most of every opportunity, because the days are evil" (Ephesians 5:15).

How you spend your time is important to God and important to you. The Bible gives us a warning here; it says be careful how you live. That means not only what you do and where you go, but how much time you spend doing certain things. When we spend too much time doing one thing in life, we get out of balance. If you spend too much time studying, you turn into a schoolie; if you spend all your time working out, you become a jock; and if you spend all your time in the video arcade, you become a burned-out video junkie. None of those are very good options for healthy, balanced people in life. God has a better idea. School is important, and so are sports, and so is recreation like video games. The important thing is that it matters to God whether you waste time in your life or not. Look back over the last several days. What's the one activity you've spent the most time in—sports, studying, having a good time? If your life is out of balance and you're spending too much time having a good time, studying, in sports, or maybe kissing your girl friend, ask God to help you bring your life back in line. He's willing and able to help you live a life in which you spend time on the right things.

FREEDOM

> **"**I have a ten-speed bike but it's not like getting the car. There's something about getting the car that's a real ticket to freedom.**"**

There's no doubt about it, getting the family car or buying your own car *is* a real ticket to freedom. There's hardly any other place in the world where the car is more important than in America. Our lives revolve around our ability to jump in the car and zip down to the corner store or over to the stadium. Sometimes people at your age don't have all the freedom they'd like when they do get the car. Lots of parents are very strict. They lay down the law, and that's when trouble starts. Most teenagers figure they're old enough and responsible enough to drive a car. But every time parents hand out the keys, lots of questions are going through their minds. *Is he going to do 70 in a 30 tonight? Will he drive the car like a sensible adult?* In the end, all their questions are basically addressing the same issue: *Can my son handle the freedom that a car represents?*

Freedom is a great thing; it gives you choices in life to go places and to do things. But freedom, like the family car, has to be handled carefully, otherwise you end up in a huge accident. The Bible puts it this way: "You, my brothers, were called to be free. But do not use your freedom to indulge the sinful nature; rather, serve one another in love. The entire law is summed up in a single command: 'Love your neighbor as yourself' " (Galatians 5:13,14).

God made you as a person to be free. God never intended for you to be bound up by a sinful habit or trapped by certain friends who you know are pulling you away from what's right. God made you to be a free person, not so you could use your freedom to do whatever you want, but so that you could do good things for people in your life. The Bible puts it this way: "Love your neighbor as yourself." In other words, obey the speed limit, don't honk your horn on a quiet street, stop at red lights. Those are small courtesies you can do to show that you have the freedom in the car but that you know how to use it. All throughout your life there are going to be speed limits, quiet streets, and signal lights. You have the freedom to respond in every one of those situations however you like. But God asks you to make choices carefully in life so that you don't take freedom and hurt others and yourself with it.

NO FREE LUNCH

23

"If God punishes sin, then why does it seem like some people always get away with the sins they commit?**"**

In your life, you have probably met people who have gotten away with things that you got caught doing. There's always somebody somewhere who sneaks off from doing some prank just before the cops come, or someone who lives the way he wants to most of the year but occasionally "makes things right with God" when he feels guilty. Some people just seem to have a knack for getting away with things. While it looks like people get away with sin, there really is no such thing as a free lunch in God's world. Everything in life has a price tag attached to it. Lots of times, the church has oversold the cost of sin. "If you masturbate, you'll go insane." "If you go too far on a date, sex will never be the same." "Anyone who has a beer ends up an alcoholic." Lots of well-meaning Christians have built walls around things in life that God never intended there to be walls around. It is true, there is a cost associated with sin in your life. When you go too far on a date or get drunk, tell a lie, or speed in a car, somebody somewhere pays for that sin. Lots of times, it's you.

When you sin in life, you feel guilty, and when you feel guilty it hampers you from seeing life clearly. Lots of times sin makes you lose time in life. You spend time doing the things you want to do to gratify your own desires and after they're satisfied a sense of hurt or pain sets in. Your self-image is tarnished. It's good to know that when you go to the Lord, He can forgive you for your sins. In other words, He can give you a sense of forgiveness so that you don't have to carry that load of guilt around with you. It is true that sin does scar people, but most scars in life won't hinder you from living a normal life. They do remind you, however, of a time when you were hurt. You need to think twice about some of the choices you're making when it comes to sex, telling the truth, shoplifting, drinking, and so on. The Bible says, "The one who sows to please his sinful nature, from that nature will reap destruction; the one who sows to please the Spirit, from the Spirit will reap eternal life" (Galatians 6:8). In other words, God has made it clear in the Bible that when you sin, the end product is hurt, guilt, loneliness, and a loss of self-worth.

The Lord never intended for you to carry those guilt feelings around with you. That's why God cautions you in this verse to be careful what you do with your life. God wants you to have as few scars as possible in life, especially the deep scars that come from the sins you know you shouldn't commit but you go ahead and do anyway. God can help you and protect you from big mistakes. And He can forgive you when you have made big mistakes. If you're on this side of some big mistakes in your life, ask God to make you sensitive to His Spirit when you're tempted. If you've made some mistakes you regret today, go back to God and let Him know that you thank Him for His forgiveness. Then let the scars remind you not of the times in your life you failed, but of the times God's goodness brought healing.

SWEATY PALMS

24

"The only thing worse than asking a girl out is giving a speech in front of the class. I hate being shy, but somehow I can't help it.**"**

Any guy who's ever asked a girl out knows the symptoms; your palms sweat when you go to pick up the phone, you stutter, and even though she can't see you, you still feel your face burning because you're blushing. Feeling insecure about asking a girl out on a date is really pretty normal. Most guys face that feeling. When we're feeling insecure in life, or shy, it's often because we don't know if we measure up to another person's standards. We're uncertain whether another person thinks we're normal or weird. Maybe you want to ask a girl out but haven't found the courage to do so, or maybe you want to get involved in sports but are afraid of failing. The Bible says, "The Lord is my strength and my shield; my heart trusts in him, and I am helped. My heart leaps for joy and I will give thanks to him in song" (Psalms 28:7).

It's great to know that God will strengthen you and help you when you trust Him. One of the great things about being a Christian is that God wants to help you with the simple things of life like shyness. God has given you a unique set of gifts and abilities. He understands that when you feel shy or inhibited in a group of people, it's hard for your real self to shine through. Next time you feel shy, stop and ask God for some of the strength He's promised to give you. Stare a person right in the eyes and let them know that you've got confidence in Someone bigger than yourself.

25 A TOUGH DECISION

"Sometimes I masturbate. I've tried so many times to be self-controlled, and every time I lose the battle. It really gets discouraging.**"**

Masturbation is one of those subjects that everyone knows about but few people talk about. For some reason, it's a private part of life and most everyone is uncomfortable talking about it. Lots of Christian guys wonder whether masturbation is right or wrong. The trouble is, when you go to the Bible, there's very little, if anything, written about it. One thing we do know is that people don't go blind or insane just because they masturbate. Yet at the same time, most people feel guilty afterwards and wonder whether it's right or wrong. Because masturbation is an intensely personal issue, it's tough to lay down the law and say it's absolutely right or wrong, especially when the Bible doesn't even talk about it. Some Christian psychologists say masturbation is a gift from God. Others say it's one of those habits—like smoking—that everyone is better off avoiding. Whether you feel masturbation is right or wrong is really between you and God. No one can legislate and tell you exactly how to live your life. Some of your decisions in life will be based on the quality of your relationship with God. Here's something to think about. God doesn't want any habit controlling our lives. The Bible says be self-controlled. In other words, don't let any physical desire overpower you to the point that it controls how you behave or what you think. Another thing God doesn't want in your life is lust. The Bible says, "But among you there must not be even a hint of sexual immorality, or of any kind of impurity, or of greed, because these are improper for God's holy people" (Ephesians 5:3).

If masturbation is coupled with looking at dirty pictures or replaying tapes in your mind of some sexual fantasy, it would be pretty tough to say those things don't have a hint of sexual immorality. They do, and God says they are improper for you. Another thing: the Bible says, "Finally, be strong in the Lord and in his mighty power" (Ephesians 6:10). God is anxious that you develop self-control in your life because He knows self-control will keep you from sins that are going to hurt you in life. When the Bible says be strong in the Lord and in His mighty power that means rely on God's strength to get you through tough situations rather than relying on your own strength. God wants you to be very careful how you live. Only you can settle the question about masturbation. The important thing to remember is that God loves you right where you are and He understands the struggles you have with your sexual feelings. Ask God to show you what He wants for you in this area. If you feel comfortable, talk to your parents or an adult about it. The important thing is, don't carry around a load of guilt that you don't need to carry around. God can give you the wisdom and the strength you need even in this intensely personal area of your life.

GOOD TIMING

26

66Sometimes I feel like my whole life is out of sync. I can't seem to catch up or to show up on time for anything anymore.99

Good timing is one of the essential ingredients in life. It affects everything we do. Belching out loud in church is not exactly a demonstration of good timing, nor is having your girl friend's father tap on the car window just when you're kissing her good night. Good timing is important in life. Here's what God's Word says: "He has made everything beautiful in its time. He has also set eternity in the hearts of men; yet they cannot fathom what God has done from beginning to end" (Ecclesiastes 3:11).

Lots of times we get in a rush. We expect our parents to understand us on our time schedule. Sometimes we try to cram too much into our school day and end up rushing to classes or studying for tests over lunch. Actually, God never meant for man to rush around. He has put enough hours in a day to do the things He has called us to do. So when we find ourselves too busy, it really becomes a matter of whether we're doing too many things, some of which maybe God isn't asking us to do. Good timing in life comes from having a balance of the right ingredients in our lives. If we're busy doing the wrong things or too many things in life, it's possible for our timing to get out of sync. God has a better idea. God wants us to be in sync with the people around us, with ourselves, and most importantly with Him. To do that, we have to do two things: (1) Trust in His judgment, even when He seems slow to bring something to pass that we think is important. He has our best interests in mind. (2) Evaluate all the things we're doing in our lives and decide which ones are really important.

If you find yourself running out of time every day and as a result feeling out of sync with everyone and everything in your life, maybe it's time to take an inventory of all the things you've got going. God wants to orchestrate your life. But to do that He needs the time He deserves so that He can work His good and perfect plan, in your life.

27 TWO FACES

"Hypocrisy stinks. I hate it when somebody is two-faced with me.**"**

Hypocrisy *does* stink. It's disgusting when somebody is two-faced and changes his values or conversation depending on what group he's with. If you've ever filled out an application for a job you've seen a space for character references. Potential employers are looking for people who come with good recommendations about their honesty and their desire to do the right thing. God asks you to be a man of character. You know better than anyone your own tendency to drift away from good habits, from neatness, or from honesty. It's not easy to be a Christian especially if you try to do it on your own strength. The Bible says, "You must have accurate and honest weights and measures, so that you may live long in the land the Lord your God is giving you. For the Lord your God detests anyone who does these things, anyone who deals dishonestly" (Deuteronomy 25:15,16).

Thousands of years ago, God told the Jewish people that He wanted them to be honest and have high standards. Sometimes we think we can get away with letting our standards slip a little. After all, who sees you on your date with your girl friend or hears you fudge the truth a little? When God asks you to be a man of character, He's asking you to be the same person when you're by yourself and the only one who knows what's going on, as you would be if God Himself were there or your best friend or your parents. That's the true test of character, being the same person day in and day out. It's having friends from different circles but acting the same with all of them. It's being just as nice to your dad when he's too strict about the car as you are to your girl friend. In a word, a man of character is a man who has a steady and honest personality. He's a man God can count on to help other people throughout life.

28
WHEN YOU SHOOT TOO HIGH

"I'm shooting high in everything I do. I think if I have high enough standards in who I marry and what job I take, I'll make it.**"**

There is something in every one of us that appreciates good quality and high standards. In fact, pursing high standards is what makes good soccer players, good gymnasts, and good debators. Shooting high is one of the best qualities you can have in life. High standards help us not settle for second best.

But there's a difference between having high standards and pursuing perfection in life. In a nutshell, life is messy. There are no perfect people or perfect jobs or perfect colleges or perfect situations. Just like there's no perfect pizza or perfect Big Mac; there's always one piece of lettuce or a mushroom missing, too much ketchup, or not enough relish. Life is like that. Often when you look at magazine ads or television commercials you see people who are nearly perfect—they dress perfectly, they talk perfectly. Beautiful women in advertising never have zits, bad moods, or body odor. It's an unreal world that we are surrounded by in advertising and entertainment. The Bible says, "There is not a righteous man on earth who does what is right and never sins" (Ecclesiastes 7:20). There is no person on earth who doesn't have faults or sin in his or her life. Even your mom and dad, as hard as it may be to see sin in their lives, still struggle with sins just like you do. Every person comes with a blueprint in life. You have a family background, hurts, problems, and sins that make you an imperfect person. Everyone around you in your life—your brothers, your sisters, your parents, your cousins, your friends at school, the preacher—comes into life just like you do, with imperfections. Imagine all these people in life, with these backgrounds full of variety, but all with flaws. Now is a good time in your life to stop thinking you'll ever find a perfect wife, or the perfect marriage, or the perfect college, or the perfect car. Perfection in this world that is so crazy simply doesn't exist.

TWO-WAY STREET

29

"I just have quit talking to my parents. I'm sick and tired of getting the third degree every time I turn around."

Do you know anyone who doesn't have hassles with his parents? Can you name one person who gets along perfectly with his parents? If you know someone who always gets along with his folks, you know an exceptional person. Getting along with parents is sometimes a big chore. It's a proven fact that parents often ask too much of their teenagers. They give lectures and criticize you. Sometimes they violate your privacy by walking into your room without knocking; maybe they listen in on your phone conversations or open your personal mail. When your parents do these kinds of things, they are wrong, there's no doubt about it. But basically, their motives are good. They're concerned about you. They love you and want to be sure that you're making good decisions in life. They don't want you to make mistakes that will take a long time to get over.

If you are a Christian, God asks that you love your parents. You don't get the same rights that your non-Christian friends have to tell your parents to go to hell or to walk out on them. The Bible says, "Love is patient, love is kind. It does not envy, it does not boast, it is not proud. It is not rude, it is not self-seeking, it is not easily angered, it keeps no record of wrongs.

Love does not delight in evil but rejoices with the truth. It always protects, always trusts, always hopes, always perseveres" (1 Corinthians 13:4–7). Here's the standard that you can measure your relationships with your folks against. Most teenagers would say they get along best and can talk best with their moms. Talking to dads is a little harder, there's no doubt about it. But communication is a two-way street. If you feel that your parents are giving you too many lectures or always giving you the third degree, or not respecting your privacy, sit down and have a talk with them. Don't go just on your feelings and lash out at them. One of the tests of your maturity is how well you show your love. Don't underestimate your parents' ability to handle an adult conversation with you. Think about it. How loving have you been with your parents lately?

SELF-WORTH

30

❝I've never had a real honest-to-goodness date in my whole life. I can't help thinking maybe there's something wrong with me.**❞**

Feeling worthwhile in life is not a feeling everyone has naturally. Sit alone on a bus once or twice, stay home alone a couple evenings, or never go out on a date, and it's easy to wonder whether you're worth anything. It seems like the people who have a lot of worth are the ones in the center of things, the ones who get the lead in the school plays, the guys who win the races, or who date the cutest girls. It hurts when you feel like you're not worth as much as someone else. The Bible says, "Do you not know that your body is a temple of the Holy Spirit, who is in you, whom you have received from God? You are not your own; you were bought at a price. Therefore honor God with your body" (1 Corinthians 6:19,20). Here in these verses is some encouraging truth. Can you imagine the God of the universe putting into your body His Holy Spirit as your comforter and guide? If you weren't worth anything, do you think God would put something as valuable as His Spirit in you? If you weren't worth something to God, would He have sent His Son to die on the cross? While God knows you and you're not a stranger to

God, you've never met Him face-to-face. Can you imagine dying for someone you've never met face-to-face? That's exactly what God did. He paid a big price for you. And, He has given you unique qualities that no one else in the whole world has. And He's given you a job to do. In your life there are many people who need you and the love you can give. Next time you feel worthless, stop and think of all the good things God has done for you. God paid a big price for you when He sent His Son, Jesus, to die on the cross. While there are some days you may not *feel* valuable, that doesn't change the fact that you really are.

GETTING RESPECT

31

"My parents make me come in by eleven on weeknights. I can't believe it. They treat me like a kid. It's the same thing at school. I even need a hall pass just to go to the john!**"**

Respect. Here you are in your late teens and your parents and the people at school still want to treat you like a kid. Why do they do that? They'll give you a license to drive a car, but then make you bring that car in at midnight. They'll let you check books out of the library, but make you carry a slip of paper when you go to the john. There's no doubt about it. Adults have some crazy ideas about respect, especially when it comes to teenagers. How do you handle it? Here's some good advice. "Therefore, prepare your minds for action; be self-controlled; set your hope fully on the grace to be given you when Jesus Christ is revealed. As obedient children, do not conform to the evil desires you had when you lived in ignorance" (1 Peter 1:13,14).

Most people your age do deserve respect, but how do you get it? Do you earn it? Is it given to you? In these verses from the Bible, two pieces of advice are given. First, be self-controlled. Most adults who have earned the respect of others have demonstrated that they are self-controlled in any situation. Maybe if you feel you deserve respect, your parents and those around you need to see your self-control in the way you drive a car or handle your brother.

The second piece of advice is, don't conform to the evil desires you had when you lived in ignorance. Sometimes parents worry whether you can handle yourself with friends who have different values than you have. As you show them that you have your own mind and your own convictions and can stand up to people with different values, respect naturally follows. The important thing to keep in mind is that getting respect is not something that will happen overnight. It's a process. As you show yourself being self-controlled and able to handle yourself in any situation, your parents and those around you will give you the respect you deserve.

32

CLOSET
CHRISTIANS

"I'd say most of my friends at school don't know I'm a Christian. After all, who says you have to broadcast it anyway?**"**

Do you hide being a Christian? It's easy to do, especially when you think you look funny, when the stakes are high, or you're afraid you might get laughed at. Faking it, when it comes to knowing God, is really pretty simple when you get down to it. With the right pair of jeans, saying the right things, and laughing at all the right jokes, it becomes easy to blend in and not be known as a Christian.

Here's what the Bible says about faking it. "A fortune made by a lying tongue is a fleeting vapor and a deadly snare" (Proverbs 21:6).

Hiding the fact that you are a Christian is like telling a lie. Like putting on a mask to cover up what is really underneath. As a result, people around you who need the same peace and hope and direction you have as a Christian never see it. There's a difference between flaunting your Christianity and simply *living* differently. When you put a mask on, you are generally trying to do one thing—be accepted by as many people as possible. The Bible makes it clear. You might gain popularity for a short time, but in the long run you'll have to come back and sort out who you are and who you belong to. God has a better idea. By not putting the mask on in the first place, you'll save yourself a lot of confusion.

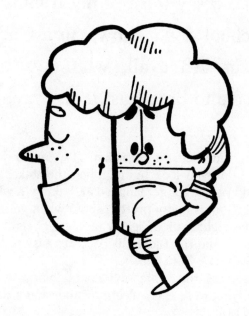

WHAT COUNTS?

33

"Sometimes I feel trapped in life. I go to school and the kids there seem like they're having such a good time. Then I go to my youth group and everybody just sits around and looks at each other. Being a Christian can be a real drag sometimes.**"**

Does that sound familiar to you? Do you ever wonder what really counts in life? Whether perhaps it's the Christians who are missing out on a good thing in life, not the people who don't know God. It's easy when people around you are having a good time to begin to think that maybe you're missing out on something. There's no doubt about it, some of the movies you see and shows on television sure make drinking and sex look like easy fun.

Thousands of years ago, another man had the same dilemma. He wanted to know what really counted in life. So he went on a journey, and he took a close look at partying, working hard, sex, getting rich, education, being young, even the weather. And in the end, he came down to two things that he said really counted in life. "Now all has been heard; here is the conclusion of the matter: Fear God and keep his commandments, for this is the whole duty of man" (Ecclesiastes 12:13).

That's it! Can you believe it? The man looked the whole world over—at everything that's important to you—and in the end he came down to two things: Fear God and keep His commandments.

Your world is changing rapidly. There are lots of voices out there to tell you what's important. For those who know God personally, fearing God and keeping His commandments have to rank up there as two of the most important things in life. Why? Because when we do those two things, everything else in life—sex, parties, weather, education, being young—takes on the right and proper perspective.

WINNING OVER SIN

34

> **"**I hate it when I sin. I feel like a first-class jerk. I wish I knew some kind of formula that would help me win over sin.**"**

You can't believe it. Just yesterday you were in church, and here you are, one day later, kicking yourself in the butt because you told a lie to your parents about a dent in the car. You didn't mean to lie intentionally, it just seemed to slip out. Some days it probably seems almost impossible for you to do the right thing all day long. Here's what the Bible says about sin and how to win over it. "For this very reason, make every effort to add to your faith goodness; and to goodness, knowledge; and to knowledge, self-control; and to self-control, perseverance; and to perseverance, godliness; and to godliness, brotherly kindness; and to brotherly kindness, love. For if you possess these qualities in increasing measure, they will keep you from being ineffective and unproductive in your knowledge of our Lord Jesus Christ" (2 Peter 1:5-8).

Winning over sin is never easy. In fact, if you think you'll win over sin by winning two or three battles, think again. Winning over sin is a process. It happens as you grow older and as you get to know God better. In these verses, we have a list of several qualities that will help you win over sin. Goodness—a desire to do the right thing; knowledge—knowing your limit on how many kisses you can handle; self-control—saying no to a joint; perseverance—saying no twice, sometimes three times; godliness—spend some time talking with God; brotherly kindness—not being selfish; and love—having respect for other people and their property. These are not qualities you gain overnight, but they can grow in you. As you and God walk together, He can show you how to develop some of these qualities in your life. Ask Him to help you develop them. You'll find that your batting average will go up, and you'll begin to win more battles over sin than you lose.

CAFETERIA BLUES

35

"Walking to school alone I can handle, but eating alone in the cafeteria, that's the pits. I can't think of anything worse in the school day.**"**

You whip through the lunch line, picking up the school district's version of spaghetti, plunk down your change, and come strolling away from the cashier. You scan the whole cafeteria; all your friends are eating with someone else. There's no choice; you've got to eat alone. In a word, it's tough. And every time you have to eat alone, it hurts as bad as the time before. It seems like the whole world stares at you, and you're sure they're thinking, *This person has no friends. He must not be too cool. Either that, or he's a schoolie."* You lose your appetite. You didn't want that spaghetti anyway.

Eating alone is tough for everyone, whether it's a woman whose husband has died, someone in college, or you in high school. It's rarely fun to eat alone. For some reason, people put talking and eating together, and when you take the talking away, sometimes food just doesn't taste as good. Did you know that when you eat alone, God cares about that? He sees you when you're lonely, and He also wants to help you with your perspective on what's important in life. "Then Jesus said to his disciples, 'Therefore I tell you, do not worry about your life, what you will eat; or about your body, what you will wear. Life is more than food, and the body more than clothes' " (Luke 12:22,23).

Obviously, you have to worry about what you eat and what you wear to some extent. Jesus didn't mean for you to go hungry and naked. He had a different idea. What He was trying to tell His disciples was that they needed a different perspective, that food and clothing are important in life, but the real meaning and importance of life doesn't come from food and clothes. It comes from knowing God. That's worth remembering the next time you have to come into the cafeteria and eat alone. It's not fun at the time, but there are more important things in life to be concerned about.

"Sometimes I wonder if this whole God and Christianity thing is for real when you can't see it. It's hard to believe in something you can't see.**"**

More and more in today's world, people question what they can't see. Television has played a trick on us: We have come to believe that we can see anything, and what we can't see must not be real. And it *is* hard to believe in things you can't see. Christianity, like most religions, tries to explain life's purpose. Like other religions, it tries to answer questions: Who are you? Where are you going? What will happen to you when you die? Answering these questions is what religion is all about. Even in the end, after you have answers to these questions, you still need one more ingredient to make Christianity come alive—faith. "Now faith is being sure of what we hope for and certain of what we do not see. This is what the ancients were commended for" (Hebrews 11:1,2).

Faith is what makes religion real. It's what makes it visible. There is lots of proof in the Bible and outside the Bible that Jesus Christ lived, and died, and rose again, but in the end you need faith to make the Bible and Christ come alive. Faith is taking the Bible at face value and staking your life on it. Like

83

the Bible says, this is what many ancient people were commended for doing. The biggest proof we have that Christianity is all for real even when we can't see it, is the fact that when people turn to God and turn their lives over to Him, good changes happen in their lives. Bad habits are broken, discouragement is turned into hope. No religion anywhere can give you answers to all of your questions. We live in a world that has both seen and unseen parts to it—a natural side and a supernatural side. Through faith, knowing God can be less of a mystery and more of a reality.

"You can tell me life is fair. But that's really tough to believe when you watch your own dad walk out the door, headed to sign up for unemployment.**"**

A month ago, your family was pretty normal. Your dad had a steady job, Monday through Friday, and your mom kept the home going. Now, one month later, what you've been reading about in the newspapers has finally hit your own home; your dad has lost his job. You can't believe it. If there ever was somebody who was truly faithful and a hard worker, surely it is your dad. The system seems screwed up. Why would he of all people lose his job? And the big hassle is how things are at home. There's tension in the air; everyone can feel it at the supper table or later on in the evening. It's like the littlest problem is magnified a thousand times. Today's economy has no respect for people. Our country is going through changes. Every company is involved with computers and information—and the people who move that information around have become the majority of the work force today. It used to be that people who worked in steel mills or were laborers made up the majority, but not anymore.

What does God say about unemployment or losing your job? Does He care? Is there any help? Here's one thing the Bible does say: "Trust in the Lord with all your heart and lean not on your own understanding; in all your ways acknowledge him, and he will make your paths straight" (Proverbs 3:5,6). If you listen to some Christians today, you'd get the idea that good Christians don't lose their jobs or don't hurt or have troubles in their families. It's not true. Nowhere in the Bible does it say that Christians will be protected from hurt. What the Bible does promise is that in the midst of hurt, God will be there. If your dad has lost his job or you know somebody's dad who has, you know there's hurt involved. It's when times are tough that it's hard to take God at His Word. Yet, in this verse from Proverbs, it says that when we trust God, He will make our paths straight. Do you realize that while it may take some time, God can make a path straight between your dad or your friend's dad and another job? It's that way with any hurt in life. When you trust God, in other words, pray and talk to Him about everything— all your feelings, all your hurts—and leave the results to Him, then God can make sense out of the crookedness and craziness in life.

If your dad has lost his job, this is a good time in life for you to be extra patient. In fact, it's a good time to be a friend to your dad and mom. They need your support now more than ever, until God provides more work and makes the path straight between your home and a new job. Trust Him, pray, and leave the results with an all-knowing God who has your best interests in mind, even though at this moment it might not seem that way.

38 HARD PEWS

"Church can be so boring. I really don't know what the big deal is about showing up every Sunday.**"**

Sunday morning church. Here we go again: two hymns, prayer, announcements, offering, the solo (which, as usual, is off-key), and then the sermon. You know the order of the service by heart. Lots of times it seems like the preacher is really tough and hard, especially on teenagers. Your mind drifts off, you begin thinking about the movie you saw last night, or the test you have to study for, or somebody you'd like to go out with. You snap back to reality, then you feel guilty inside for not paying better attention. You think, *I'm getting absolutely nothing out of this service. Why come to church anyway?* It's a good question. Why go to church, especially on those days when it's not everything it's cracked up to be?

Jesus had something to say about that: "For where two or three come together in my name, there am I with them" (Matthew 18:20). Believe it or not, the reason you should go to church is not because it looks good, or because your parents say you should, or because society says it's a good thing to do, or out of habit. Jesus promised that when people came together to talk about Him and to study His Word and to worship Him, He would be there. The reason we go to church today is we need to go to one place on a regular basis where we, along with others, can meet God. It's imporant to meet God on a regular basis. Somehow, the discipline of going to church not only makes Sundays more meaningful to families, it also provides a structure in which we can find answers to some of life's tough questions. Granted, there's repetition in church. Somehow, we might think that church should be as interesting as television or the movies. Many times it won't be; it's not designed to entertain us. It's more like school in that it's designed to teach us and to help us with life's problems. Some Sundays church *is* boring. If you have a good idea about making church more interesting, why not share it with your pastor? Next time church is a drag, remember: Church is one place God promised to be. When you show up, so will He.

❝Does God really expect me to give a tithe on the little bit of money I make doing odd jobs?❞

Money questions. What part of your allowance or part-time job money belongs to you? to others? to God? Do you have to give a portion of what you make to the church? How can God expect you to give a tithe on $43.50?

Anyone who knows God personally and gets an allowance or makes money on a part-time job has to deal with the issue of tithing. Think about what the Bible says in this verse: "Honor the Lord with your wealth, with firstfruits of all your crops; then your barns will be filled to overflowing, and your vats will brim over with new wine" (Proverbs 3:9,10). All throughout the Bible, there is a pattern that gives you some ideas on tithing. Generally, the pattern is this: God has done a lot for you in your life. There are many good things that have happened to you, including becoming a Christian. One of the primary reasons people tithe is that it is a way of thanking God, of saying thanks for everything He has done for them. The way they show it is to give a portion of what they make to Him. The Bible says that every good thing comes from God. It's pretty reasonable to assume that although your parents might give you an allowance or you found a job yourself, ultimately, it came from God.

The Bible says we should tithe to honor God with a portion of the good things He's given us. That means not only with our money, but with our time and our abilities as well. God didn't put us in this world just so we could make ourselves happy; He has a job for us to do. And the way He gets His work done is through us and through the money that we give to the church. God deserves a portion of what you make on a regular basis. Most people figure the portion God deserves is about 10 percent. Whatever amount you're comfortable with is between you and God. The important thing is to do it regularly. You're setting patterns now for how you will spend money the rest of your life. The Bible promises that as we give to God, His blessing will rest on our lives. That doesn't mean we can bargain with God and get rich; it does mean that in many ways, our lives will be rich and full if we honor Him with a portion of what we make.

40

FLAT BROKE

"I'm broke more often than I've got a few bucks in my pocket. I don't understand it— twenty bucks for the week down the tubes in two days.**"**

You know what happens when you spend money every time you get the urge. Bankruptcy sets in, and your allowance or part-time cash goes up in smoke. Because you are a Christian, God wants you to manage your money carefully. Most Christians know tithing is important. When we tithe, it's like saying thank you to God for the good things in our lives. It gives God some money to work with to help others. But what about what's left over? How do you handle that? The key to how you handle the money in your life is wrapped up in one word—*balance*. Here's what the Bible says: "Offer hospitality to one another without grumbling. Each one should use whatever gift he has received to serve others, faithfully administering God's grace in its various forms" (1 Peter 4:9,10).

One of the clues to how to spend your money correctly is wrapped up in these two verses. Not only does God deserve a portion on a regular basis of what we make, but other people deserve a portion also. Think back to the last twenty bucks you had in your pocket. How much did you spend on yourself? How much did you spend on entertainment, playing video games, buying pizza, going to the movies? How much did you put in the bank for college, or a rainy day? How much did you devote to doing something nice for your mom or dad or someone else? How you spend your money now will tell you a little bit about how you're going to spend it the rest of your life. You're setting patterns now. That's why it's important to exercise balance with whatever money you have to handle in your life. God deserves a portion, you deserve a portion for yourself, and other people deserve a portion. Check yourself. Watch the balance between what you spend on good times, on yourself, on savings, or on others. Ask God to help you achieve a balance that pleases both Him and you.

CHEAP THRILLS

41

"It's funny, I get started on one program, and the next thing I know, I've watched three or four TV programs in a row."

How much time did you spend this past week watching television? Add it up—two hours, four hours, six hours, eight hours, ten hours, . . . Today, the average American watches TV more than four hours each day. Since you are a Christian, does it matter to God how much television you watch or what you watch? Television is cheap fun, it's free, but just because it's free doesn't mean it doesn't cost you something if you watch too much. The Bible says, "Be self-controlled and alert. Your enemy the devil prowls around like a roaring lion looking for someone to devour" (1 Peter 5:8).

Too much television numbs your mind and after a while if it numbs your mind, it will numb your self-control, lessening your alertness to right and wrong. That's when your thought life goes crazy. One of the tests of whether you're watching too much television is to check how you feel after four hours in front of the tube. You might want to check your grades; how many important projects have you procrastinated on so that you could watch just one more show? Too much television is not good for you. It takes away your ability to interact with others, to use your head, and in the long run, it reduces your ability to resist temptation. Next time you find yourself in front of the tube for a couple of hours on end, watching one show after another, stop and think. There may be something more constructive for you to do with your time. Television is cheap fun and cheap entertainment. There are lots of good things on television today, but television, like anything else in your life, needs to be controlled. The key is control, not only in what you watch, but how much you watch.

"I'll tell you one thing, it's a lot easier *saying* God is number one in your life than *living* like He is. I don't wake up very many days feeling like I want to be a Christian.**"**

It's true. *Saying* God is number one in your life and *making* Him number one in your life are two different things. It's tough to make God number one on a day-to-day basis. Most Christians want to put God first, but when they get busy or the pressure is on, it's hard to do the right thing. Maybe the problem is that you don't really understand what God wants from you.

Here's an interesting verse of Scripture that might help you. "And Jesus grew in wisdom and stature, and in favor with God and men" (Luke 2:52). That little verse blows a lot of holes in what some Christians might tell you about Jesus and about how you should live. Notice the four areas mentioned: Jesus grew in wisdom, that means His mind, His mental ability grew; He grew in stature, that means His body grew, He grew muscles and learned how to use them; He grew in favor with God, He got to know God's Word and spent time praying to God; He grew in favor with man, that means He had friendships, He had

95

friends He spent time with. The four areas are mental, physical, spiritual, and social. Jesus Himself grew in all four areas. That means He handled temptation in all four areas too.

What does that mean to you? It means several things. One thing it means for sure is that God doesn't expect you to walk around like some kind of spiritual giant or zombi. He expects you to exercise your mind and your body and to have friends. The thing you need to realize, though, is that every area of your life will compete for attention. That means each one needs to be controlled. The only way you ever keep your mind in control and your body in control and your friendships controlled is to have one key area—the spiritual area of your life—in control, cleaned up, and functioning well. The way to do that is to know God personally and to spend some time with Him, talking with Him and reading the Bible—the guidebook for daily living. God's dream for you is balanced living. He does not want to turn you into a spiritual zombi, He doesn't want you hung up or cramped in life. God's best for you is to be free to be yourself, yet balanced in the four key areas of life. Christ was a teenager once. He knew the hassles you have every day. Next time you get in a jam or feel like your life is out of balance, take a minute to stop and talk to God, and remember: His dream for you is balanced living.

TOUGH IT OUT

43

"Sometimes my conscience bothers me when I do something wrong. Other times it doesn't. I can't figure it out."

Everyone knows what it feels like when his conscience bothers him. It's that sick feeling somewhere between your tonsils and your belly button that comes during or after the time you looked at your neighbor's paper in geometry class or lied to your parents about where you were. In today's world, having a conscience that bothers you is something most people put down. It's as if only a goody-goody lets his consciences bother him. When everyone around you feels that way, it makes it tough if you're a Christian to believe your conscience is a good thing. Actually, your conscience is a gift from God. If your parents have taught you right from wrong, they have worked to cultivate your conscience. Having a sensitive conscience actually can be a benefit to your life; it can save you from a lot of hassle and pain.

Here's something that was written in the Bible that talks about your conscience. "So I say, live by the Spirit, and you will not gratify the desires of the sinful nature" (Galatians 5:16). In that verse is a simple piece of advice—live by the Spirit. What does that mean? It means that if you want to avoid the pain and hurt that comes from sin, you'll need to pay attention to your conscience. In other words, listen to that voice inside you that speaks about right or wrong. God can talk through that voice if you're willing to listen, but sometimes it's hard to hear that voice. When it is hard to hear you'll need to do something different. And that is, simply, *tough it out.*

Toughing it out when you can't hear your conscience is one of the hardest things you'll ever do, especially when the desire to do something that'll feel good is really strong. And the only way to tough it out is to have patterns or habits in your life. In other words, a life-style that makes it easy for you to resist temptation. That life-style is something that you'll build over time if you put a little effort behind it. Ask God to help you today to be sensitive to your conscience. Ask Him to help you dig in when you can't decide whether something's right or wrong. Live that day in a way that would measure up to the standards God has set.

44

"If you really love someone, I find it hard to believe that God is going to zap you for having sex with her.**"**

How much sex is too much, especially when you love someone? This is a tough question and it deserves a long answer. When you care about someone and you have a desire to be close to her physically, a simple Bible verse like "flee youthful lusts" somehow just doesn't cut it. You need more and you know it. Sometimes it's hard to do, but on a big question like how much sex is too much, you need to try to see it from God's viewpoint.

Why do you think God made the rules about sex so strict—that sex is reserved for marriage? There are lots of reasons, but two stand out. Believe it or not, when God laid down this law millions of years ago, He had *you* in mind. God has always been committed to man and to giving man the best life possible. Sin fouled that up. One of the things sex outside of marriage does is cause disharmony in your life. Why? Because men and women are put together in such a way that they need commitment to make sex meaningful. Sex without commitment can feel good for the moment, but the deep satisfying sense of belonging to another person and being at peace with yourself is lost when you are intimate with someone outside of marriage. Commitment is important and without it, disharmony develops in your life. Disharmony and troubled emotions are not what God has planned for you. God wants to give you a life with peace and purpose. Because you are a Christian, sexual sin ties you up in knots.

First Corinthians 6:18–20 puts it this way: "Flee from sexual immorality. All other sins a man commits are outside his body, but he who sins sexually sins against his own body. Do you not know that your body is a temple of the Holy Spirit, who is in you, whom you have received from God? You are not your own; you were bought at a price. Therefore honor God with your body."

The Bible makes it clear. If you want to avoid the disharmony and the troubled conscience that comes when you have gone too far, evasive action is required. That means not going parking on those nights when you're preoccupied with your date's body. That means biting the bullet and not picking up a dirty magazine at the corner store. It means lots of little choices during the day to think differently. It's not easy; God never promised it would be. But if you're willing to do your part, God is committed to forgive you when you fail and to keep strengthening you when you ask Him, so that you can win the next battle.

STARTING OVER

❝I'm so tired of starting over and over and over. It seems like every time I turn around, I have to ask God to forgive me for the sin I committed yesterday.**❞**

For young Christians, starting over and over and over and asking God to forgive them repeatedly for the same sin is a way of life. It just seems like some things can never be beaten. For sure, masturbation is one of them. Changing an attitude is tough, too. Here's what one man wrote about the frustration of starting over and over. "So I find this law at work: When I want to do good, evil is right there with me. For in my inner being I delight in God's law; but I see another law at work in the members of my body, waging war against the law of my mind and making me a prisoner of the law of sin at work within my members. What a wretched man I am! Who will rescue me from this body of death? Thanks be to God—through Jesus Christ our Lord!" (Romans 7:21–25.) These verses are some of the most sensible ones in the whole Bible. They're realistic and they were written with you in mind. Even holy, good people like Paul struggle with sin. There are some sins in life that, because of your background or personality, are tough to beat; you don't win over them easily. So how do you handle that?

The key is to learn to accept the war in your life. All of your life you are going to wrestle with sin. You need to remember that somehow what Christ did on the cross, while it's a mystery and hard to figure out, makes you able to win over sin. But because you're human, you will not win over sin every time. That doesn't mean you get sloppy or lazy and say, "One more time won't hurt; God will forgive me." That's taking advantage of the good things God has done for you. Rather, the goal is to work at getting your batting average up, so that more and more your life is pleasing to God and to others.

46

TWO MASTERS

"I can't say I'm totally happy as a Christian or totally happy when I don't act like a Christian.**"**

Lots of people suffer from the mistaken illusion that they can be Christians most days but once in a while act like they don't know God when they want to have a good time. It doesn't work. If you're looking for an unhappy life, one surefire way to find it is to be a Christian on Sundays and a hell-raiser the rest of the week. The problem with trying to be a Christian and a non-Christian at the same time is that you end up having two sets of values depending upon what feels good at the time or who you're with. The result is you get torn up inside.

The Bible puts it this way: "No one can serve two masters. Either he will hate the one and love the other, or he will be devoted to the one and despise the other. You cannot serve both God and Money" (Matthew 6:24). If you have two sets of values in life, one of them will eventually win out. Your mind and your emotions can't handle the stress of being a Christian one day with one set of friends and doing things that are against God's Word on other days with another set of friends. God put you together in such a way that it's just not possible to walk with God and have ungodly values at the same time. God's way of doing things says that you work toward one goal: walking *with* Him or walking *away* from Him. The Bible says if you're double-minded (have two sets of values) you'll be unstable in everything you do. Take a minute and think about it. Are you a Sunday Christian? Does how you talk, the jokes you laugh at, or what you do depend on who you're with? God has a different idea. The more consistently you try to do what is right, the more contented you'll be and the more meaning you will find in being a Christian.

47   A TRUE FRIEND

"Sometimes in church they talk about the Holy Spirit. It gives me the creeps. It sounds like a ghost or something."

Who is the Holy Spirit anyway, and why do we get uncomfortable sometimes when the Bible or the preacher talk about the Holy Spirit? Actually, it's quite normal to have questions about the Holy Spirit. Lots of people do. When you live in a real world where you can see and touch things every day, it's tough to believe in and talk about someone you can't see. Here's what Jesus said when He was on earth: "And I will ask the Father, and he will give you another Counselor to be with you forever—the Spirit of truth. The world cannot accept him, because it neither sees him nor knows him. But you know him, for he lives with you and will be in you" (John 14:16,17).

One of the greatest things God has ever done for you is that He put an unseen Counselor on earth to help you in every situation. Frankly, this is mysterious, and it's not easy to explain. But stop and think about it. Who is it that brings Bible verses to mind in your life? When you're tempted and you hear a voice that says, *Don't do that,* or *Be careful,* did you ever stop and think about where that voice came from? The Bible says you can't see the Holy Spirit, but He's in the life of everyone who is a Christian. He can give you advice, and He can comfort you and convict you. The Bible says God's Spirit even translates our prayers when they just don't seem to come out right. The easiest way to explain the Holy Spirit is to describe Him as an unseen Friend in your life. While He's hard to explain and the world won't accept Him, that doesn't make Him any less real. The next time you read about the Holy Spirit in your Bible, or your pastor says something from the pulpit about Him, don't panic over the religious talk. God's Spirit, your Friend, is in your life to help you and guide you.

48 HISTORY IN THE MAKING

"What's the big deal about what happened on the cross at Calvary? It's so hard to believe in an event that took place two thousand years ago."

For Christians, there's nothing more sacred than what happened on a small hill just outside of Jerusalem two thousand years ago. The fact that a man named Jesus died on a cross two thousand years ago is generally accepted by most historians. And lots of other sources besides the Bible talk about a good man named Jesus who claimed to be the Son of God. That doesn't change the fact, though, that occasionally even Christians wonder about the cross and why it is so important today.

Here's what the Bible says about why the cross is important today. "Day after day every priest stands and performs his religious duties; again and again he offers the same sacrifices, which can never take away sins. But when this priest had offered for all time one sacrifice for sins, he sat down at the right hand of God" (Hebrews 10:11,12).

In simple terms we could put it this way: Man screwed up. After Adam sinned, God set up a sacrifice system so that when man sinned, he could go to a priest and the priest could offer a sacrifice that would cover up the man's sin so God wouldn't see it. From God's point of view, though, that was pretty much a temporary system. Something more permanent had to be done because the more men that came on earth, the more sin there was and the harder it was to cover up the sin so that God couldn't see it. Some kind of a major sacrifice was needed. That's why God sent His Son, Jesus, to become a man and to die so that one death could, in a symbolic way, cover all the sins of man.

You know the rest of the story. Not only was it important that that man, Jesus, die on the cross, but it was equally important that He come alive again to prove that man could live again and live forever if he believed in the cross and what God did for him there. That's a lot of heavy stuff, but just because it's heavy doesn't mean it's not true. You could read a lot of history books or religious books about God and Christ and the cross. But the best proof for believing Christ actually died on the cross and rose again is found in the lives of people who once didn't believe and then believed. The change in their lives is radical and that is just how God promised in His Word it would be. How about you? What do you believe about the cross and what Jesus Christ did for you there? Has what you believe changed your life?

49

WHO IS JESUS?

"Sometimes I'm not sure I believe Jesus Christ really was the Son of God. That's a pretty fabulous claim when you think about it.**"**

In today's world, we tend to trust and believe in the things we can see or push a few buttons to control. Most people believe that you control the destiny of your life and that the events in your life—what happens, where you go, who you marry, what college you go to—are all up to you. The Christian thinks differently. When Jesus was on earth, He asked His friends this question: " 'Who do people say the Son of man is?' They replied, 'Some say John the Baptist; others say Elijah; and still others, Jeremiah or one of the prophets.' 'But what about you,' he asked. 'Who do you say I am?' Simon Peter answered, 'You are the Christ, the Son of the living God.' Jesus replied, 'Blessed are you, Simon son of Jonah, for this was not revealed to you by man, but by my Father in heaven' " (Matthew 16:13–17).

For some reason, it is very, very important to God that you decide who Jesus Christ was. Was He simply a good man with good ideas who went around trying to help poor people? Was He a lunatic? Or was He the Son of God? If we were to see the world from God's perspective, there are really only two groups of people: those who believe Jesus was the Son of God, and those who don't. Obviously, if you believe Christ was the Son of God, then you are living a certain way. You'll live differently than those who don't believe it, simply because of what Christ has done in your life. You know Christ asks you to read and follow the Bible. Lots of people never really come to know Jesus Christ because they fear they have to give certain friends up, that knowing Christ will cramp their life-styles, that it's sissy stuff, or that they'll have to give up good times in life. If you feel that way, you're really misinformed. There are millions of people who have lived before you, or who are alive today, who believe Jesus Christ was more than a good man or a good teacher. They believe He actually was the Son of God. Those people have come to know that Jesus Christ can be their Friend, that He can teach them how to live right and while that's a mystery in their lives, they know that life is better now than it was before they believed in Jesus Christ. The dividing line between people who know God and those who don't know God is simply how they answer the question: Who is Jesus Christ? How about you, who is Jesus Christ to you?

WALK ON

50

"After I came back from church camp last summer, things went really great for about two weeks. Then I hit the skids. Being a good Christian was really great for a time, but now it seems like I can't do anything right."

One of the biggest misconceptions Christians have today is that if you're a good Christian, then your life is one constant high and you move from one big event to another. Some of the most unhappy and dissatisfied Christians today are those who buy into this. The fact is, knowing God is more like a spiritual journey. It's not moving from one big event to another, it's a process.

"All these people [Abel, Enoch, Noah, Abraham] were still living by faith when they died. They did not receive the things promised; they only saw them and welcomed them from a distance. And they admitted that they were aliens and strangers on earth. People who say such things show that they are looking for a country of their own. If they had been thinking of the country they had left, they would have had opportunity to return. Instead, they were looking for a better country—a heavenly one. Therefore God is not ashamed to be called their God, for he has prepared a city for them" (Hebrews 11:13–16).

The Bible talks about certain people—Abel, Noah, Abraham, Sarah, and others—who were friends with God. They realized life was a journey. They realized that life had peaks and valleys in it, that there were good days and bad days.

In today's world, some Christians believe that they are not good Christians unless their lives are going smoothly and God answers all their prayers. Knowing God and walking with Him is not one constant high or one constant low. Making things right with God at summer camp or at a weekend retreat and then coming back and struggling is really quite normal. You can't live your whole life at a retreat. The real test is how you live when you come back. In the real world, success and failure walk hand in hand. If you find that your life has spiritual highs and lows in it, relax. God understands you, your personality, and the challenges in your life, and He loves you today just the way you are. The more you consider your relationship with God as a journey and as a process, the more at peace you'll become with what it really means to be a Christian.

QUIET TIME

51

66My daily devotions are about as regular and predictable as a pop quiz.**99**

Having a regular quiet time is something that lots of Christians struggle with. In fact, some would tell you that unless you read your Bible and pray an hour a day, there's something wrong with you spiritually. That's not true, and unfortunately, people sometimes feel guilty when they don't measure up to such a standard. God never intended for your time with Him, whether you're reading the Bible or praying, to be a drag or boring. And, He didn't give us the Bible so we could memorize verses that don't apply to our lives. God has a good idea for you when it comes to reading the Bible and praying. Jesus put it this way: "Watch and pray so that you will not fall into temptation. The spirit is willing, but the body is weak" (Matthew 26:41).

There's no doubt about it, your walk with God will take some time. You can't eat at McDonald's all the time and stay healthy. They can broil it, fry it, freeze it, chill it, and kill it, but it's still fast food. A good diet takes time to prepare and time to eat. The same is true of your walk with God. Stop and measure your daily devotions over the last several weeks. Maybe you've been just "driving through" for your daily devotions. Jesus put it straight. When you pray and watch for God, or in other words, take some time on a regular basis and read your Bible, you'll protect yourself from a lot of hurt that comes through giving in to temptation. Maybe you need to read your Bible where it's quiet, but the great thing about knowing God is that you can talk to Him anywhere, at any time. In fact, God would rather hear from you while you're in the swimming pool or walking home from school than hear from you only once in a while on your knees or when you're in church. The more you think of daily devotions as time spent with a Friend and not something you have to do every day for a certain period of time, the more encouraged you'll be about what it means to really know God and walk with Him.

52

IMPRESSIONS

"Everyone in my school is so hung up on impressions that they act phony just to have certain friends."

How to leave a good impression is not something most people sit around in the cafeteria and talk about. But everybody's thinking about it. Guys check to see if their zipper is up. People put Clearasil on zits. Some people run extra hard just to win a race. Others go to the library and study rather than go to the cafeteria and eat alone. And everyone seems to be so worried about who they are seen with in the halls. Our world is overly sensitive to how people look. Leaving a good impression is almost more important nowadays than what a person's really like. Good impressions are important to a point. If you were to try to get a part-time job in a bank as a teller and you applied for the job dressed as a punk rocker, it's not too likely that you'd leave the right impression. Good impressions are important when it comes to looking for a job, meeting new people, and so on. When you become too conscious of what clothes you are wearing or who you're seen with, then you actually are struggling with pride. Here's what God told Samuel when Samuel was looking for a king. "Do not consider his appearance or his height, for I have rejected him. The Lord does not look at the things man looks at. Man looks at the outward appearance, but the Lord looks at the heart" (1 Samuel 16:7).

It's never easy to see life the way God sees it. For some reason, God is forever seeing life from a different point of view than you. When you read in the Bible that God forbids some things, like getting drunk or hating someone, you tend to figure God is restricting you. In reality, God is only trying to protect you from deep hurt. The same is true when it comes to impressions. It's hard to see people from God's point of view. For some reason, it's much easier to look at the outward appearance and make a judgment about a person's worth than it is to look on the inside. That's why crippled people or ugly people sometimes make you uncomfortable. It's hard to look inside a person when the exterior shell isn't as pleasant as you often wish. What really counts in life is how people think, what they believe in, what their values are, whether or not they're sensitive or open and willing to grow. All of these qualities are internal and they only show themselves once in a while. As a Christian, you know better than to judge people just on their outward appearances. God's Word tells us so. God's Word says we should look more deeply at people than just how pretty their skin is. Other people's value (and in fact, your value) comes from inside.

HE'S IN CONTROL

53

❝Why does my pastor always say I have to die to self? That makes being a Christian sound so strange and heavy.**❞**

Die to self. What a worn out, old cliché that is. Somehow we always identify that cliché—die to self—with preachers, stick-in-the-muds, and most everyone who forgot what sex is really like. It always seems these are the people walking around saying you've got to die to self. Actually, when the Bible uses the term *die to self,* it has something entirely different in mind than what some Christians might tell you. Dying to self as a way of living is a legitimate concept when it's correctly interpreted.

Here's what the Bible says: "I have been crucified with Christ and I no longer live, but Christ lives in me. The life I live in the body, I live by faith in the Son of God, who loved me and gave himself for me" (Galatians 2:20).

That verse sounds heavy but actually here's what it means. Some of us are way too alive to ourselves—our own passions, our likes and dislikes, our dreams and fears. If you really want to live, you need to die to the *too aliveness.* In other words, there's nothing wrong with good, healthy, normal desires in your life, but there are times you are too alive, you are overly stimulated by the things you want in life. Wanting to be physically close to another person is not a sin, but when that occupies all of your thinking, then you become too alive to something you want. That's when the Bible says to slow down. The Bible says that's when to ask God to help you be not so alive to the things you want in life. God has never once been against man's normal desires. God put the desires in your heart for closeness to another person, for joy, for happiness, for success, for winning. God wants you to be alive in life but not so alive that you are driven to do things that in the end will hurt you.

WHAT IS FUNNY?

54

❝What do I think is funny? I guess I'd say cutting other people up is funny.❞

What's funny to you? Have you ever gone out with a group of friends and the whole conversation ends up being one big, fat, sarcastic joke on somebody in the group or someone left behind? Let's be honest for a moment. Most teenagers don't really know how to laugh at good jokes. Much of the time, teenagers laugh at somebody else's expense. Sarcasm and cutting somebody up is like standard operating procedure. In fact, lots of people give unseen rewards to the guy who can cut someone else down the best. Poking fun at people, dirty humor, ridiculing somebody with a handicap, or mocking out adults can all be funny but that doesn't make them good jokes. The Bible says, "Brothers, do not slander one another . . ." (James 4:11).

It's not easy when you're just one person in a larger group to steer the conversation away from cutting somebody down, but since you are a Christian, God asks you to set an example even among your Christian friends. It's easy to slip into cutting somebody down, being sarcastic, and as a result, hurting a person or their feelings. Check yourself. What have you been laughing at lately? Are you laughing at someone else's expense? God wants you to laugh and enjoy life, but not at the expense of others. Ask Him to help you be sensitive to what you laugh at so that you're building other people up rather than tearing them down.

"HAVE FAITH"

55

"I heard a preacher on television say once that all I needed to do was to have faith in order to get ahead in life. Is that true?**"**

Often you'll hear preachers, Sunday school teachers, and well-meaning Christians say to people who are down and out, "Just have faith. If you had faith, your life would be different." What does it really mean to have faith? Does it mean you go and do far-out things like jump out of airplanes without parachutes? Does it mean you take chances dating a non-Christian for a long time believing that she'll eventually come to know God? The Bible says faith is being sure of what we hope for and certain of what we do not see. Lots of people in the Bible were commended for having faith. The Bible also says that without faith, it is impossible to please God. It's important to have faith. But the most important thing to remember is, "Because of the Lord's great love we are not consumed, for his compassions never fail. They are new every morning; great is your faithfulness" (Lamentations 3:22,23).

Having faith is something you work at all your life. Your value and worth in life are not dependent on how much faith you have in a given situation. God's willingness and desire to be faithful to you far outweigh all of your personal struggles with faith.

56

GOD'S WILL IN LIFE

"How can I know the will of God for my life? Sometimes it seems so hard to find something that big."

Knowing God's will is important if you're interested in God's best for you. Sometimes we throw the term around, "it's the will of God" or "know the will of God." When somebody is hurt or dies, people often explain it away by just simply saying, "It's the will of God." All the tough questions, the hurts, the disappointments, are not so easily explained away simply by saying, "It's the will of God." There's something about *the will of God* that sounds cold and unbending, like God isn't flexible—either measure up to His will or you get zapped. Lots of these misconceptions about God's will have come from Christians and not the Bible. Here's what God says to us in His Word: "Teach me to do your will, for you are my God; may your good Spirit lead me on level ground" (Psalms 143:10). The writer of those words, King David of Israel, had the right idea when it came to God's will. David had a friendship with God and he realized that he had a lot to learn from his Friend. He also realized that knowing God's will or doing God's will was not something he would do naturally. That's why he asked God to teach him. In other words, knowing God's will for your life is like going to school; it takes time to get all of the learning you need.

You don't learn God's will for your life overnight. When it comes to knowing what school you should go to or who you should marry or what direction you should take in life, knowing God's will is more often than not a process, it's a series of events in your life more than a zap of lightning or a vision in the middle of the night. Simply put, God's will is His plan of action for you. Because God knows you better than anyone else—even better than you know yourself—you can trust Him and His plan of action for your life.

57 GETTING GROUNDED

> **"**My parents grounded me because they say I mouthed off to them. Sometimes their punishment is out of line for the way I really act.**"**

Can you think of anything worse than being grounded? Being grounded is exactly like prison at home. And what makes it worse is that usually we feel like we've been unjustly punished for something we didn't think was that bad. The thing that makes grounding painful is that it takes away our freedom, it cuts us off from the outside world and the things we do that make life enjoyable. It used to be that parents just pulled out the belt and in a few moments a good whipping was over. Nowadays, grounding is more popular. Whether your parents make you write long sentences over and over, ground you, or hit you, the reasons are always the same, even though the method is different. Parents who love their children discipline them when they do something wrong. The Bible says, "My son, do not despise the Lord's discipline and do not resent his rebuke, because the Lord disciplines those he loves, as a father the son he delights in" (Proverbs 3:11,12).

There's a difference between discipline and punishment. Punishment is a strong response to injustice. Discipline, on the other hand, is a corrective response to help a person think clearly and avoid making the same mistake twice. Any discipline such as grounding is designed to help you think clearly. Most of the time when parents discipline you, they do it because they love you, not because they're out to hurt you. Some discipline takes away your freedom. But there's a reason for that. We all need to be reminded occasionally in life that when we overstep ourselves and speed, come in late, or tell a lie, we're actually infringing on the rights and freedoms of someone else. Getting grounded is never fun, but it does do the job. Another important thing to remember is that as much as it seems crazy to do so, you should thank God for your parents who discipline you. There are very few things that parents can do that show you any more love than discipline.

> **"I fail to see how rock music is bad for you. I haven't gotten in trouble yet and I listen to it all the time."**

If you've ever watched "Solid Gold" on television, you've heard their closing theme song. It has a phrase in it about the music "taking control." That's an interesting phrase when you think about some of the songs big groups are putting out these days. Anyone who says that the lyrics and music don't affect him is denying reality. Rarely are words put to music just to support the beat. More often than not, music is wrapped around words to deliver a certain message. As Christians, we need to stop and think occasionally about the music we listen to. Unfortunately, today's music is a mixture of both good and bad, just like the movies. One group may put out three or four great songs and then come up with a real raunchy one, or one that says live your own life the way you feel. God doesn't expect you to run away from today's music, hide your head in the sand, and listen only to Christian music. What He does expect is balance in what you listen to. The Bible says, "Wisdom will save you from the ways of wicked men, from men whose words are perverse, who leave the straight paths to walk in dark ways, who delight in doing wrong and rejoice in the perverseness of evil, whose paths are crooked and who are devious in their ways" (Proverbs 2:12–15).

In these verses the Bible warns us that there are wicked people. It's funny, isn't it, to think that some of the groups we see on television or at a concert could be called wicked. God's Word says that if we have wisdom we can avoid these people who are going a different direction than Christians are going. There are two ways to have wisdom when it comes to the music you listen to. The first one is balance. Rock, classics, blues, jazz, Christian music, all of these are legitimate forms of music that deserve to be listened to. If you're listening to only one kind of music, you might want to stop and ask yourself why.

The second way you can have wisdom when it comes to music is to ask yourself whether you can turn the radio on and off at will. Do you need the radio on every time you get in the car or every time you're in the house alone? How do you feel after you've listened to an hour and a half of rock? What do you think about? Does the music honor God? It's not likely that God expects you to give up rock music. What He does ask is that you be careful about the messages those songs deliver and about letting them control or dominate your thinking and your life. Listening to a variety of music and having control over the music in your life will go a long way toward helping you offset the negative influences that many songs bring.

59 SPIRITUAL DRYNESS

"Sometimes I go through periods in my life where I feel really dry as a Christian. I don't want to read my Bible, God seems far away, and I feel like being a Christian about as much as I feel like being the Pope.**"**

Spiritual dryness is not a sin nor is it a sign that God has left you. When some people first become Christians, they have a real sense of God's presence in their lives. Then, not too long after that, they seem to drift away from God or at least feel as if God is drifting away from them. Even old saints of the church feel spiritually dry sometimes. It seems like an illness, like catching a cold. It just sneaks up on you. If you ever feel spiritually dry, the important thing to remember is that your Christianity and walk with God is not measured by how you feel. Rather, it's measured by what you do and what you believe. Lots of Christians believe because they feel close to God or feel like Christians, that makes them Christians. It's not true. Knowing God has its peaks and valleys just like the rest of life. When you know God's forgiven you for some sin you've committed, it's natural to feel close to God. But there are other times after you've studied for two or three tests for finals week or you've had a fight with your mother or you've been sick, when it's normal to feel as if God has drifted away from you.

When spiritual dryness comes into your life, you need to stop and look at how others responded to God in their lives. Here's what the Bible says about Abraham: "Was not our ancestor Abraham considered righteous for what he did when he offered his son Isaac on the altar. You see that his faith and his actions were working together, and his faith was made complete by what he did. . . . You see that a person is justified by what he does and not by faith alone" (James 2:21,22,24). Here in these verses is encouragement for getting through times of spiritual dryness. The Bible says that if you have faith in Jesus Christ as a Christian, but never act like you're a Christian, you basically have a dead religion. Sometimes for very good reasons, our religion gets dry. That's when we need to ask ourselves whether we're operating just on faith or whether we've just been too busy to spend time doing the things God has asked us to do. All through your life, spiritual dryness will come and go. That's when it's time to take inventory. Have you been too busy, sick, tired, frustrated? Have you had a fight with God and you're not talking to Him? Is there sin in your life? If any of these conditions exist, then you have faith without action. Simply saying you're a Christian, but not taking the time to read God's Word to get to know Him better or to spend time in prayer with Him can account for that spiritual dryness. The same thing in reverse can happen too. We can get so busy working as Christians, reading our Bibles, praying and acting like Christians, that we don't stop long enough to simply pray and rest in God, in other words, have faith in Him. Next time you experience spiritual dryness, check your life out to see whether it's in balance. As you bring faith in God and the right activities together—prayer, Bible study, and balanced living—that spiritual dryness will go away.

"I love getting down with my friends and boogying to records or going out for pizza. There's some nights I feel like I could stay out all night."

The "good-times spirit" in your life can be a real asset to you if you channel it right. It seems that in every person there's a spirit of wanting to get down or stay out all night or boogie. That energy is healthy, and because you are a Christian, God can use that energy not only for your good and enjoyment of life, but He can channel it into useful and productive activities that will help people. That's what dedication of your life to Christ is all about. But once in a while, that energetic spirit in you can turn into wildness. And like wild horses, that spirit can drag you all over town before it lets up on you. A writer in the Bible puts it this way: "This only have I found: God made mankind upright, but men have gone in search of many schemes. . . . No man has power over the wind to contain it; so no one has power over the day of his death. As no one is discharged in time of war, so wickedness will not release those who practice it" (Ecclesiastes 7:29; 8:8).

Oftentimes people are driven by pursuit of good times. They're on an endless search to break free from the boring life they live, to find something that feels good. Lots of times that energetic spirit turns into a wild spirit and that's when people get into trouble. Believe it or not, banks are robbed, people are murdered, women are raped when the wild energy in a person takes over. Sometimes Christians are confused and feel as if God doesn't want them to have a good time in life. Sometimes we think energetic Christians aren't as holy as laid-back Christians. Like so much of life, God asks us to try to maintain a balance between good, healthy energy and a wild spirit that burns up energy but takes us nowhere. Ask God today to show you whether you've gone in search of many schemes, whether or not you're driven by a wild spirit that's taking you nowhere. God can help you channel your energies so that you can get the most out of life and yet honor and please Him.